FAM

FIRS
FAT

FAMILY MATTERS

✓

FIRST TIME FATHER

SEAN CALLERY

WARD LOCK

First published 1991 by Ward Lock
Villiers House, 41/47 Strand, London WC2N 5JE, England

A Cassell Imprint

British Library Cataloguing in Publication Data

Callery, Sean
 First time father — (Family matters)
 1. Fatherhood
 I. Title II. Series
 306.8742

 ISBN 0–7063–6952–1

Typeset in 11 on 11½ point ITC Garamond Light by
Columns Design and Production Services Ltd, Reading

Printed and bound in Great Britain by
William Collins & Sons, Glasgow

CONTENTS

INTRODUCTION

Being a father is fun. It is also worrying, distracting, exciting, exhausting, fulfilling . . . the list goes on and on. Becoming a father is a new job for a man, but unlike other jobs he gets minimal training and guidance, while his mistakes are pointed out frequently and loudly. Nobody said it was going to be easy, but sometimes it feels as if you don't stand a chance!

There are countless books about pregnancy on the shelves, but look up 'father' in the index and you find only a handful of entries: men are in many ways excluded from it. Yet pregnancies and child rearing go better when the man is closely involved. This book is designed to help men through the process of becoming a father. It gives advice on how to plan for a baby, what happens throughout pregnancy (to your child, your partner, and you), the birth, and coping with a new baby and a new perspective on life.

There are three key practical points to consider:

1. **Communication:** Talking things through with your partner is the lifeblood of the relationship and the foundation of your future security.
2. **Housework:** If you don't already do some of the cooking, cleaning and washing in the household, now is the time to start. It will help your partner get through pregnancy without becoming over-tired, and

will be a positive contribution to the relationship.

3. **Baby care:** From the 2,000 nappies that will be changed in a year, to feeding, washing and playing with a new child, men are more involved in the practicalities of parenthood today than ever before.

But fatherhood goes deeper than this. The role of the father has changed very rapidly in recent times. As recently as 20 years ago the idea of him attending the birth of his child was considered unusual, and his role in the family was wage-earner, occasional playmate and chauffeur. Now at least seven out of every ten fathers witness their baby emerging into the world (and not merely as an observer, but as a birth assistant), and many men make great efforts to spend as much time as possible with their child. The whole family benefits from this: the parents' relationship, the child's development, and the man's personality. Today it is acceptable for a man to put his family first in a way that would have been considered wimpish 20 years ago.

Coping with these changes, taking on these new roles, handling new emotions, however, does not come easily to men. During a pregnancy a man can become jealous, resentful and frustrated at his partner — and then feel guilty about having such thoughts. Women are supported throughout pregnancy by a team of doctors, midwives, hospital staff, and women friends in a way that men are not. Every father has emotional and perhaps physical reactions which he has to recognise and cope with.

This book takes a prospective father through some of the experiences he will undergo, and offers reassurance and guidance to help him enjoy the time of pregnancy and his new role as a parent. I interviewed many first-time fathers during my research, and nearly all of them made the same comment: 'I really enjoy it, and I wish I had worried less'. I hope this book helps you worry less during this important new phase in your life.

Chapter 1

DECIDING AND CONCEIVING

Let us first of all examine the questions that will come up when choosing to have a child. We are lucky to be able to make the choice these days: a couple of generations ago people had less access to reliable contraception and starting a sexual relationship often meant starting a family. The decision to create a new human being will have repercussions for the rest of you and your partner's life. How do you weigh up the pros and cons? Or do you act purely on instinct, and say 'We just want to have a baby'.

MAKING THE RIGHT DECISIONS

The most important consideration is that this should be a decision that you and your partner make together. It may be either of you who raises the subject first — to the surprise, or perhaps the relief, of the other.

There are, however, several reasons why men are often reluctant to start a family:

★ No wish to change lifestyle — maybe you are very happy with your world as it is.
★ Drawing back from the commitment represented by having a child together.

★ Worries about the cost of running a baby combined with probable loss of income by the mother.
★ Fear of the unknown.
★ Not ready for the responsibility of fatherhood.
★ Not enough room in your house or flat.

However, a number of positive factors may also influence you, and you may not be aware of them beyond realising you have an instinctive yearning to be a father.

★ The life force: every species has an urge to reproduce.
★ The prospect of parenthood, seen as a source of joy.
★ The desire to be a family, to create a tiny community of your own.
★ If your relationship is not going well, the hope that a baby will bring you together.
★ Parental pressure to produce a grandchild for them.
★ The time seems right.

You will most likely agree with some points for and against the idea. It may be worth writing down your feelings, or perhaps you may like to ask yourselves the following questions:

★ Are we confident we could make a child happy by providing a secure and loving home?
★ Have we got enough space for the baby to have a sleeping area and eventually its own room, plus space to store all the vital equipment such as pushchairs, toys, clothes.
★ Can we afford a rise in expenditure combined with a fall in income, however temporary the fall is?

TALKING IT THROUGH

Once you've thought about these questions, then both partners will need to talk about their feelings. Make time for this when neither of you is tired (not in the middle of the night) or has to rush off somewhere with the subject still in the air (say, at breakfast). Both of you must make an effort to be honest and to listen to each other. This could be the first time you have spoken so openly about your feelings with one another, and that is something to be pleased about because it will strengthen your relationship. One thing to watch out for is whether you are saying 'I want a child' or 'I want a baby boy/girl'. If you both agree that you would like a baby, when secretly you are only interested in having one of a certain sex, you stand a 50/50 chance of being disappointed. Specifying the sex of the child you want brings into question your motive for wanting a child at all: do you want to create a new life, or are you trying to find someone to fulfill the dreams you never achieved.

IS THE TIME RIGHT?

It may be that you both agree you want a baby, but are concerned about the timing. This may be the case if you are not earning enough on your own to support a wife and child, or need to save more for a deposit on your own home. Perhaps one of you recently took on a more demanding job that is going to take up more time, making pregnancy and a child inconvenient at the moment.

If you are considering moving house, move now or leave it until the baby is born: moving during pregnancy causes great strain. You will also want to discuss points such as whether your partner would intend to return to work after the birth, and if so who would look after the baby (you? a childminder, relative or nanny?).

WHAT HELP CAN YOU GET?

Depending on who you talk to, babies are either remarkably cheap to run, or a constant and forceful drain on your finances. You can get some financial help from the state:

★ If your partner works, she is probably entitled to Statutory Maternity Pay (SMP) from her employer for up to 18 weeks.

★ Mothers who cannot receive SMP are entitled to Maternity Allowance from the state.

★ If you or your partner are receiving Income Support or Family Credit, you may be allowed an extra Maternity Payment, which is a one-off sum for each baby expected.

★ Child Benefit is paid for every child you have.

★ Family Credit is a benefit for working families with children, the amount depending on income, number of children and their ages.

★ Income Support is benefit to help people who do not have enough money to live on, even if they are working (for up to 24 hours a week).

★ If you receive Income Support, you are entitled to free milk and vitamins for your partner and your baby.

★ Families receiving Family Credit or Income Support can claim for travel expenses to and from hospital, including trips before the birth.

Enquiries about benefits should be made to your nearest Social Security Office, Child Benefit Centre or family Credit Unit.

PRE-CONCEPTUAL CARE

If you are united in your wish to have a child and agree the time is right, the next step is to prepare to conceive a baby. Before you stop using contraception, there are a number of things to do.

1. If your partner previously had a miscarriage or abortion, she will probably want to talk to her doctor, who will advise if there are any likely problems in her conceiving again.
2. Your partner should also ask her doctor to check that she is immune to rubella (German Measles) as the baby could be damaged if she is not and she catches it during pregnancy.
3. If either of you has incidents in the family of inherited conditions such as Down's Syndrome, cystic fibrosis, haemophilia, talk to your doctor. You may be referred to a genetic counsellor who can guide you on the chances of the condition being repeated in your child.
4. Healthy parents are most likely to produce healthy children. Your body will make more healthy sperm if you are fit. Do not allow your testicles to get too hot: it may be worth stopping wearing tight, constrictive clothes, and taking a shower rather than a long hot bath.
5. Your partner should cut down her alcohol intake, and certainly stop smoking if she can. Both would threaten the baby's health. This applies to men as well. Passive smoking may affect your partner and alcohol can affect the health of your sperm.
6. If your partner is past her mid-30s, there is a higher risk of having a Down's Syndrome baby. The risk of one such birth in every 2,000 to mothers aged 20 rises slowly to one in 885 at age 30, one in 109 at 40, and one in 12 at 49. If your partner is at the older

end of the range there are tests that can be done to check this during pregnancy (see page 31).

7. If either of you has had a sexually transmitted disease (STD), such as herpes, you should both have a check up with the doctor before trying to conceive. Some STDs are carried by both partners but only show symptoms with one of them, hence the importance of you both checking.

8. If your partner is diabetic she may need special treatment during pregnancy. Consult your doctor.

9. If either of you work with or near dangerous chemicals or radiation (say, from X-rays at the dentist or in a hospital) it may affect your fertility. If you are not sure, ask your doctor.

10. If either of you is HIV positive, and thus a potential carrier of the AIDS virus, you must consult your doctor before conceiving.

CONCEIVING

Conception is not as easy as you may think. Considering all the warnings we are given about the importance of contraception when we start to have sex, it would be reasonable to assume that making love without contraception inevitably leads to pregnancy. This is not the case.

Women are only fertile for a few days each month in the middle of their menstrual cycle. Midway through the cycle ovulation occurs when an egg is released from the ovary and starts to travel down the Fallopian tube towards the womb. It is at this time that conception may take place. Once fertilised, the egg will implant itself in the lining of the womb and begin its life as an embryo. To accurately judge the best time, your partner should be aware of the midway point of her menstrual cycle (days 13–15 of a 28-day cycle, or 14–16 or a 30-day

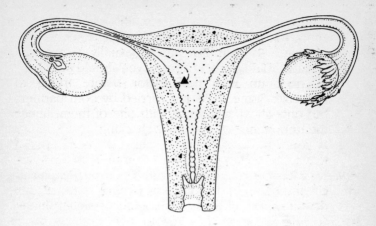

Fig. 1 The female reproductive system, showing the two ovaries, one of which produces an egg each month. This passes through the fallopian tube to the uterus.

cycle). She may prefer to monitor the rise in temperature that occurs at ovulation with an ovulator test kit available from most chemists.

If your partner has been taking the responsibility for contraception and was using the coil, her doctor should remove it. If she is on the Pill, it may take a few months for her body to adjust when she stops: the Pill prevents conception by making the body behave as if it is already pregnant.

Psychological pressure is a strange thing, and nothing is more of a passion killer than a sense that this act is a duty to be performed for some other purpose. So do a little planning to ensure that you make love at the best time for conception, but that it happens fairly naturally.

GIRL OR BOY?

Some couples take measures to try and increase the likelihood of conceiving a boy or a girl. It is dangerous to take these too seriously as the birth of a baby of the 'wrong' sex will be very disappointing, but provided you treat it in a light-hearted manner, there is no harm in having a go. Some women adjust their diets, with lots of salt and meat for a boy, and dairy products such as milk and cheese for a girl. Still others make love just before ovulation for a girl, and after it for a boy.

PREGNANCY TESTS

As she will be the person to discover the pregnancy, your partner may get very anxious towards the time her period is due. If it starts, she may be disappointed. If it is a little late, she may have already begun to get a bit excited and will feel very let down when the mistake is realised. Try to be supportive and patient. Some women say they know the moment fertilisation has occurred, of course, this could just be wishful thinking. Your partner may start to feel sick, particularly in the morning. You may or may not be aware of this: she will probably keep her suspicions to herself until her next menstrual period does not take place.

Now she will be able to test herself for pregnancy with a kit bought from a chemist, or visit her doctor and ask him to carry out the test.

INFERTILITY

The keener you are to have a baby, the harder you will have to work to control your frustration and anxiety while you wait. Most couples have to wait a few months before succeeding (the average is 5.3 months), and one in ten take a year. If you are worried, you can consult your doctor and/or a family planning counsellor, but they will most likely suggest you try for at least 12 months before recommending any tests. Three quarters of all couples who wish to conceive do so within a year.

Men and women can be infertile for a number of reasons, both physical and psychological, and the condition can be temporary. If you are concerned that one or both of you is infertile you will have to face the strain of talking about this private problem with experts. If they can solve the problem, it is obviously worth it. You will be given plenty of advice and guidance on this distressing problem.

UNPLANNED PREGNANCY

An unexpected announcement from your partner that she is pregnant can be a great shock. Don't over react — give yourself time to think about it. If you feel your partner deliberately allowed herself to become pregnant without consulting you, you are likely to feel as if you have been used. Some researchers say this is quite a common occurrence, but that will not make you happier about it. Your partner's behaviour indicates a communication problem in the relationship, and when you get over the shock, you may consider seeing a counsellor together to help you sort out why this happened. However happy you have been together up until now, having a baby will change your lives, and you should have had a right to a say in this.

Chapter 2

THE FIRST THREE MONTHS

Your reaction to the news of a baby is unpredictable, even to yourself. It may be that the enormity of the event stuns you, or you may just feel joy. It is advisable to keep this joy to yourselves for a few weeks. Some pregnancies miscarry within days of conception (indeed this can occur without the woman even being aware her egg was fertilised), and if you have broadcast the news to friends and family early, you will face some depressing backtracking. The pause before you can 'go public' with the news can be an odd time, in which neither of you will really believe conception has happened.

WORKING OUT THE BIRTH DATE

Length of pregnancy is measured from the number of weeks since the first day of your partner's last period. So if, as is likely, conception took place in the middle of the monthly cycle, and you found out she was pregnant a week after her next period was due, she would now be five weeks pregnant, although conception occurred three weeks ago. You can now work out roughly when the baby is due to be born: 40 weeks after the first day of her last period, 38 weeks after conception.

Once it is confirmed that she is pregnant, your partner will be examined by her doctor. She will be asked details of both your medical histories, weighed, and given blood and urine tests. She should stop taking any medication, unless supervised by her doctor.

WHAT IS HAPPENING IN YOUR PARTNER'S BODY

The fertilised egg has travelled, via the Fallopian tube, to the womb, a journey which takes up to four days. It is constantly dividing cells to create new ones which in turn subdivide so that by the time it enters the womb (also known as the uterus) it numbers more than 100 cells. Each carries a genetic blueprint made up of a mixture of traits from you and your partner — hair and eye colour, shape of nose, and so on. At about four weeks, it plants itself in the womb lining, called the placenta. The baby, now about the size of a full stop on this page, floats in a bag of fluid, called the amniotic sac. It will remain inside this expanding bag, warm, insulated from its surroundings, for eight months, growing and developing into a tiny human being.

The pace of growth is rapid at this stage. At four weeks, the embryo would be just visible to the human eye. A dozen days later it has grown to nearly ½ in (1.25 cm) in length, with the spine formed and the internal organs developing.

After ten weeks the foetus, as it is now known, is 2 in (5 cm) long, has most of its organs formed, and a beating heart (begun by a number of clustered cells contracting until they settle into a regular rhythm — the heartbeat, which in a foetus is about twice as fast as an adult's heartbeat). Fingernails start to appear. It will weigh 1 oz (28 grams), and is capable of moving within its protective sac, although this would not be detectable by the mother.

HOW YOUR PARTNER FEELS

The womb, a pear-shaped organ, starts to expand and at 12 weeks is about the size of a grapefruit. Your partner's body starts to increase its production of the oestrogen and progesterone hormones to support the baby. These hormonal changes are probably the cause of 'morning sickness', the nausea which in fact occurs at any time of day, and is as often just a feeling of wanting to be sick as an actual vomiting. Your partner will start to get tired very easily, and perhaps have trouble getting up in the morning. Apparently the early stages of pregnancy feel a bit like flu. All this is in complete contrast to the popular notion of pregnant women looking and feeling wonderful. With luck, however, that time is not long away.

MORNING SICKNESS

If your partner feels nauseous in the morning, try giving her a cup of tea, milk, or perhaps a cracker — anything light for her stomach to get to work on. This can help relieve the feeling of sickness. Keep some emergency rations such as biscuits, dried fruit or raw vegetables with you in the car to help her during journeys or for when she goes to work. Eating little and often, rather than three larger meals a day, may also help.

She may also find certain smells make her feel sick. Washing powder, smoke from cigarettes, food frying, coffee — it could be anything which sets her off. You can help here by removing the source of the smell if possible, or at least storing, say, the coffee in a less frequently used cupboard. As many of the nausea-inducing smells are food related, one of the most useful things you can do is cook for your partner.

Apart from being concerned about her, you may worry about the baby not getting enough food. Don't. At

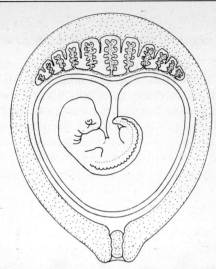

Fig. 2   The scene inside the womb early on in pregnancy.

this stage the baby is so small it needs very little nutrition. The nausea may be nature's way of getting the mother to slow down and rest.

Perhaps you are already a confident and accomplished cook, sharing the food preparation chores with your partner. Or maybe you have never touched a saucepan except to wash it up (if that!). Now is the time to learn. There are plenty of books giving good basic guidance. Starting to cook is easier than ever because now there are plenty of frozen meals, and cook-in sauces to lessen the workload.

Unfortunately, at the very time when you might enjoy the support of someone congratulating you on making a sumptuous meal, your fellow-diner at the last minute might not feel like eating — but *you* will know it was good! If you do not have one, now may be a good time to buy a microwave oven. It makes some cooking much easier and quicker, and will be useful later on when the baby is born.

COMBATING NAUSEA

1. Encourage your partner to eat little and often.
2. Keep emergency rations with you when you go out together — and remind her to take some whenever she leaves the house.
3. Store nausea-inducing foods in a separate cupboard in a sealed container.
4. Do the cooking, or at least the food preparation.
5. Keep a stock of fresh fruit juices and carbonated water which will be soothing to sip.

HER DIET

You will also want to ensure that your partner is given a healthy diet with lots of fresh vegetables and a good balance of protein and vitamins. There are plenty of good books giving advice on diet. It is worth stressing that one thing pregnant women should not do is try to slim, even if they were doing so prior to pregnancy. Their body may not be able to sustain the baby while coping with weight loss.

FOOD SCARES

The other point to make about diet is that recent years have seen a number of food scares which particularly affected vulnerable groups such as the old, and the pregnant. These food scares involved the bacteria salmonella and listeria, which can cause serious illness, even death, for your partner or your baby. It would be safe to keep pâtés, soft cheeses (unpasteurised) and raw eggs off the menu.

FOOD CRAVINGS

One of the best-known (and much derided) aspects of pregnancy is food cravings — the urgent desire to eat a specific food, sometimes in quite large quantities. Celery, pork pies, pomegranates — the craving can be for almost anything, even food which your partner previously despised. It may be caused by her body's need for a certain vitamin supplied by the food, or it could be psychologically induced: no-one really knows. All you can do is tolerate the craving, be prepared to try and find it in the kitchen at 3 a.m. in the morning if she wants it, and hope that it is not something expensive like caviar!

HER HEALTH

You should also support your partner in stopping smoking if necessary, and in keeping alcohol intake to a maximum of the equivalent of a glass of wine a day. Tobacco and alcohol can be harmful to the baby, especially in the early weeks of its development. It also would be unfair to regard your partner as the automatic choice of chauffeur for the evening if you go out and intend to drink alcohol.

Your partner will also start to change shape, particularly her breasts which will grow bigger. Some women feel very self conscious about this change in an appearance they had got used to over the years. They may be concerned that they do not look as attractive as they did — be reassuring.

Your partner should avoid lifting heavy weights as straining the stomach area could cause a miscarriage. She may have to take regular rests, particularly if she has been bleeding a little and told by her doctor to stay in bed as much as possible.

CATS AND DOGS

If you have a cat and use a litter box, you should make sure you are the one who empties it. This is because cat faeces contains a germ which can cause a disease called toxoplasmosis, which could damage the baby. If your partner continues to handle the litter, she should do it wearing rubber gloves to protect herself from infection.

If you had been thinking of getting a dog, it may be wise to delay buying the animal until after the birth of the baby. Dogs demand a lot of time, and also, a dog introduced into your home before the birth may become jealous of the baby when it arrives and could possibly harm it.

ANXIETIES

The early weeks of pregnancy are an anxious time. Inevitably your partner will have times of worry about some physical event (for example a little bleeding is quite common — and can cause fear that it is the start of a miscarriage). Both of you also face the mental stress of knowing that this is it: the baby is on its way, and in less than a year your lives will be unalterably changed. For some men, this hard reality does not hit home until later in the pregnancy. For others, the brooding starts now. Anxiety, even feelings of inadequacy and depression, are natural for anyone facing such an enormous upheaval.

Like you, your partner has to adjust to the reality of the pregnancy. She is likely to undergo some rapid and extreme mood changes through this time, and to appear quite irrational. You may find that the smiling, placid creature you left a few minutes ago is transformed into a sobbing wreck when you return — only to change again a few minutes later.

You may feel guilty about even having thoughts such as 'how are we going to cope? Have we done the right thing?'. Your guilt will be made worse by the congratulations offered to you by people as they hear the news.

However, without becoming over-sentimental about it, this is a precious time for two reasons. First, you and your partner can share the anticipation of the coming of your first child. Second, these are the last few months for many years when you will be together as just the two of you, without anyone else to worry about.

HOW ARE YOU FEELING?

Some fathers-to-be become much more interested in other people's babies at this stage, holding and cuddling them at social gatherings when before they would have ignored them. They may also start to treat pets in a more baby-like fashion. You may find your performance at work suffers as your mind wrestles with the impending changes in your life. Some men become preoccupied with thoughts about pregnancy and parenthood, and have difficulty keeping their minds on the job. Others find that they work harder, committed to doing the best they can to help make the future home as stable and secure as possible. Men are not as open about their feelings as women. The person who will be most understanding is likely to be a man who is already a father, or your partner.

Some men start to take a lot more exercise when their partners become pregnant. This may be to encourage their partner to stay fit. Sometimes it is simply part of the preparation for fatherhood. You may want to be a lively, fun-loving father who can play actively with his child. That will mean you do not want to be overweight and put in difficulty by shifting your enormous bulk across the park to pick up a ball!

Some men may even start to get symptoms of pregnancy themselves — nausea, feeling dizzy — or perhaps develop some other ailment such as toothache. Although popularly lampooned as a sympathetic pregnancy, these are probably signs of stress, anxiety about your partner and the future.

SEX DURING PREGNANCY

Once your wife is pregnant, your sex life can be focused again on pleasure rather than conceiving. That should make it more relaxed and natural, but this is not always the case. Both of you may worry about damaging the baby, however small it is, by penetration or lying on top of it. These natural concerns are unfounded and in fact you can continue your sex life in whatever way you choose without threatening the unborn child. Some women find that their libido, or sex drive, is stronger during pregnancy. This is because their body is pumping blood into the reproductive organs, which also take care of the sex drive. Fine. But not all men find this welcome at this time — the pressures of prospective fatherhood can reduce your sex drive.

Other women find the very idea of sex a turn-off and will not want to be touched at all. Enlarged breasts can be extremely sensitive and even the most gentle caress will be unwelcome. As in all aspects of parenthood, honest communication and understanding are the best way to solve any difficulty. However rejected you may feel by your partner spurning your advances, you must realise that it is not you she is going off, but the physical act of lovemaking, which she feels, for whatever reason, is not right in her condition. Sex can become a battlefield for many tensions in the relationship, some of them nothing to do with making love. This may be the first time you talk openly with your partner about sex. Try to be flexible, and remember there are many positions in which intercourse can take place, that penetration is not the only way of making love, and anyway there are many more ways of giving and receiving love than sex.

MEDICAL PROBLEMS

MISCARRIAGE

About 90 percent of all miscarriages occur in the first 15 weeks of pregnancy, and it has been estimated that one in six pregnancies is ended by a miscarriage within 12 weeks. Sometimes these miscarriages happen so soon after conception that the woman may not even be aware that she was pregnant. In the main, miscarriage is nature's way of solving a problem, whether it be a defect in the mother or the baby. Miscarriage does not necessarily mean that your partner cannot conceive again. It does mean a lot of pain, and upsetting grief for a lost life, however small. It is not easy to cope with, and both you and your partner may benefit from some specialist counselling to help you come to terms with your loss. Some men feel that the miscarriage was somehow the woman's fault. This is unfair: the cause of the problem could just as easily have been a faulty sperm.

Chapter 3

THE MID-TERM

The three middle months of pregnancy, the 'mid-term', is the time when both future mother and father face the reality of the forthcoming birth, and start to plan for it. It can be one of the happiest times of the pregnancy: women often feel at their best during this period, and men start to feel more involved in the whole process.

This can be a good time to take a holiday. Restrictions on air travel vary from airline to airline, but most will accept pregnant women up to 32 weeks, sometimes more, with a doctor's certificate confirming no problems and no multiple births.

HOW THE BABY IS DEVELOPING

After three months the foetus is fully formed at about 3 in (7.5 cm) long, with all organs, muscles, limbs and bones in place. The head is still much larger in relation to the rest of the body (foetuses look more like dome-headed aliens from space than miniature human beings), but this difference is lessened through the rapid growth now commencing — within four weeks the foetus will have doubled in length.

Within a few weeks the baby has a more human-looking face with eyebrows and eyelashes, and it is developing its own fingerprint. At about 20 weeks the baby is as long as it will be at birth, but weighs only 8 oz (226 g), so from now on it fills out. It will move around enough for the mother to notice a shifting sensation. The movements may increase into kicks which can catch the mother unawares and feel like someone booting her insides about. The baby's heartbeat is now audible via a foetal stethoscope — or, with a bit of experimentation on the positioning, through an empty toilet roll.

WHAT IS HAPPENING IN YOUR PARTNER'S BODY

The middle three months should, with luck, find your partner with restored energy and a glow of health. If she has a job, she should be perfectly able to carry on working throughout this term if she chooses. She will still be subject to some rapid mood changes, and some women get very broody, depressed and anxious. The mid-term is also a time when some women have a tremendous 'nesting' instinct. They may frantically make up for the neglected housework of the last couple of months (unless you did it), and will make a special effort to clean and tidy the house.

Early in this period your partner will probably gain a discernible 'bump'. She may be quite proud of it (in private at least) and you may like to cup your hands round it, placing them centimetres from where your child is floating. Her breasts will continue to expand and if she did not do so before, she should start wearing a bra. She will also find that some of her clothes no longer fit, and will start wearing loose fitting or elastic-waisted garments.

ULTRASOUND

At about four months, the hospital makes a scan of the baby to check on its development and positioning. The scan will also reveal if there is more than one foetus in the womb! This is an event well worth attending if you can, even if you do not intend to be there at the birth. As the ultrasound waves scan the body, there on a monitor screen you will see your baby for the first time. Many hospitals are able to supply a photograph of that moment, so if you cannot be there you will still have a chance to see it. A lot of parents mark this as a key moment in the pregnancy, when they see concrete evidence of the tiny being in the womb.

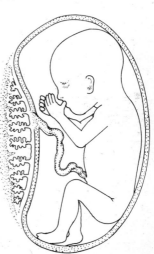

Fig. 3   The foetus at 16 weeks.

ANXIETIES

Fear that the baby is deformed is common to both parents during pregnancy. It is especially strong (rightly) if there is a history of inherited disability in either family.

AMNIOCENTESIS

Testing for abnormality is usually done at 14 weeks but carries risks of its own and raises the issue of what you would do if it shows a deformity. You should be clear on this before the test takes place: if you would want to continue with the pregnancy anyway, there is no need to undergo the risk of the test. If you would want to abort the baby, action would have to be taken fast, with little time for second thoughts. This is a question you must discuss with your partner before the mid-term, as the tests are made early in the pregnancy. Women over the age of 35 are statistically more likely to produce a baby with a chromosome abnormality such as Down's Syndrome, and the risk increases with age (see page 14). The test involves removing amniotic fluid from the womb with a fine needle. It carries a risk of inducing miscarriage in about one out of 100 cases.

THE BIRTH PLAN

It is during this period that you should both start making some of the important decisions about the labour, including issues such as what drugs your partner is prepared to accept. These decisions are often grouped together and referred to as the 'birth plan'. Items in the birth plan include:

1. Choice of home or hospital birth, and if the latter, which hospital.
2. Whether the father will be at the birth.
3. Likely position and environment for giving birth (see pages 35 and 32).
4. Which drugs or medical treatments are acceptable and under what circumstances (see pages 54–55).
5. Whether your partner wants to breast feed.

The first choice you face is whether to have a home or hospital birth.

HOME BIRTH

Because of their location, home births tend to be less tense, regimented occasions than those in hospital, and if he wishes the father is much more involved in the process — he cannot be excluded from his own home! The woman is in a familiar, controllable environment and is free to move about as she pleases. However, many women are particularly nervous about their first labour and may prefer to opt for the constantly available medical support of a hospital.

HOSPITAL BIRTH

Hospitals are strange establishments, identified with sickness rather than the joy of new life. They are equipped, however, with the latest technology to monitor the progress of mother and baby, and if staff are sympathetic, a hospital birth can be a happy and secure occasion. Fathers tend to feel out of place at the hospital, at least at first, and obviously a journey will be necessary every time you want to see your family.

WILL YOU BE AT THE BIRTH?

Fashions and attitudes change. Twenty years ago it would have been unusual for a father to be present at the birth of his child. Birth was women's business, carried out in sterile rooms (albeit under the direction of a man). Times have changed. The majority of fathers now attend the birth, some, it has to be said, under duress. It is worth deciding now if you would like to be present, because over the next few months you can practise with your partner some of the ways you can be useful to her during the labour.

REASONS NOT TO BE THERE

Some men are very definite in their decision not to be at the birth. Among their reasons are the following:

1. They would not be able to make a useful contribution — in fact, they could get in the way.
2. They can't stand the sight of blood. What could be worse than fainting during the event itself!
3. They would get upset at seeing their partner in pain.
4. They would distract their partner, who would be concerned about them rather than herself.
5. They won't be able to get there in time.

That last point raises a serious problem. Although your partner has probably worked out the date when the baby is due, such calculations are highly inaccurate. A tiny minority of births take place in the predicted week, let alone the specified date. Many are early, but about 70 percent are late, sometimes by a couple of weeks. Clearly it is impossible to book leave in advance for the event. Even if your employer is flexible and understanding about you taking a few days off at short notice, it may not be possible when the time comes.

REASONS TO BE THERE

Many fathers decide they would like to be present at the birth of their first child and their reasons include:

1. They want to share the joy of being the first human beings to see their new child.
2. They want to share the experience with their partner.
3. They can help their partner, interpreting her wants, helping her to breathe properly — generally giving support.
4. She insists he should be there!

THE SUPPORT TEAM

You and/or your partner will come across a number of professionals during this period. They may not explain who they are and what they are doing (senior doctors and consultants in particular can be guilty of this). If in doubt, do not hesitate to ask them what their role is.

MIDWIVES care for the mother and baby before, during and after the birth. Community midwives care for the mother during her pregnancy, visiting her at home and being available at the antenatal clinic. They also keep an eye on the baby once it is brought home. If the labour is not complicated, it will be under the control of a midwife at the hospital.

HEALTH VISITORS are nurses who work in the community, and give help and advice on babies and small children.

GPs are general practitioners — doctors — and are a good point of contact for basic guidance and checks, and of course the first 'professional' to confirm the pregnancy.

OBSTETRICIANS are doctors trained to deal with medical problems in pregnancy, so you will meet them if there are complications, or if you want to consult them about something.

OBSTETRIC PHYSIOTHERAPISTS are specialists in getting and keeping the body fit for pregnancy and recovering afterwards. Your partner may or may not need such help.

If your immediate reaction is that you would find the whole process bloody and distressing, try to talk with a father who did attend a birth. Labour is a much less bloody process than many men imagine, and many fathers who saw their child enter the world describe it as one of the most exhilarating moments of their life. If you stick by your choice not to attend, your partner may well opt to have someone else there to support her. This 'birth assistant' may be a friend (especially one who has children), sister or mother. Despite your decision not to be there you may feel jealous of this person, and feel they are intruding into your life. Remember, just as you have a choice not to attend the birth, your partner has every right to arrange to have whatever help and support she wants.

WHICH HOSPITAL WILL YOU CHOOSE?

It is not commonly realised that parents-to-be have a choice about which hospital to give birth in. Factors which may affect the decision include:

1. The reputation of local hospitals — perhaps one is renowned as a well-run and flexible establishment.
2. How far from home the hospital is.
3. Whether they welcome fathers into the labour ward and under what conditions.
4. Visiting hours — are they long enough for you to visit after work or for long periods?

CHOOSING THE POSITION FOR GIVING BIRTH

Your partner will be thinking about how she wants to give birth. The traditional image of the woman splayed out on a hospital bed is far from the norm nowadays. After all, logic suggests it should be much easier to give birth standing or squatting, because gravity helps instead of hinders the movement of the baby. Some of the different methods in giving birth are detailed in the chapter on birth later in this book (see pages 58–61): at the moment, your partner will want to gather information about the options. Take an interest, because some labour positions rely on support from a person — you!

BREAST FEEDING

Your partner will be asked quite early on in pregnancy if she intends to breast feed the baby. You may be surprised at how you feel if she opts to try to breast feed. Many men get quite possessive about their partner's breasts and do not like other males looking at them. So the prospect of your partner popping out a breast in some public place to feed the baby may unsettle you. Even breast feeding in the privacy of the home can make men feel jealous.

However, breast feeding is the most natural way to feed a baby: it helps it bond with its mother, it is safe and convenient, and breast milk is the best possible food for a baby.

BOTTLE FEEDING

Bottle feeding uses either milk 'expressed' from the breast with a rather undignified pump machine, or manufactured milk. A major advantage of bottle feeding for a man is that he can help feed the baby. Many parents choose to mix the two methods, breast feeding during the day, and expressing milk for night feeds which can be given from the bottle by whoever is awake.

SEX DURING PREGNANCY

The point has already been made that intercourse will not harm the baby. As the woman's bump grows, such concerns are likely to be raised again. During penetration your penis cannot damage the baby because the womb is sealed with a thick mucus plug like a lump of jelly. You will need to try a variety of positions for intercourse, however, as the 'missionary' position with the man on top can be uncomfortable for the woman. There is no reason why you should not both get a lot of enjoyment out of this experimentation — provided, as discussed in the last chapter, both of you want to continue having sex.

HOW ARE YOU FEELING?

During the mid-term, while the mother-to-be has her changing body to show for pregnancy, the man has nothing. He can become jealous and broody, resenting the altered form of his partner, tired of the endless conversations with outsiders about 'baby', and anxious about the future to the point of developing physical symptoms such as rashes and toothaches. It is important not to feel guilty about this at a time when the popular image is one of anticipatory jollity. Discuss your feelings with the person most likely to understand and share some of them: your partner.

Chapter 4

THE FINAL THREE MONTHS

The final three months of the pregnancy are times of consolidation and preparation for all three people involved — the baby, the mother, and you.

HOW THE BABY IS DEVELOPING

Early in this period the baby opens its eyes for the first time. These are most likely to blue, whatever the colour of its parents' eyes. If they are going to change colour, they will do so a few weeks after birth. It responds to touch and sound — kicking in reaction to loud noises. Its kicks are now so powerful that you can sometimes see the skin on the tummy move. Rest your hand on your partner's midriff and if you are lucky you will feel one of the kicks. By 32 weeks the baby is drinking large quantities of amniotic fluid, and sometimes gets the hiccups. Some foetuses manage to suck their thumbs, and all can her their mother's voice, the gurgling of her intestines and the pounding of her heartbeat. Outside noises also penetrate the womb so music, typing, and your own and your partner's voices will be picked up. One woman trying to ensure she produced a musical child played Mozart to her baby throughout this period. The baby turned out to be bad-tempered and tone deaf!

Over the last few weeks some very fine and soft hair called lanugo has grown over the baby's body, probably to maintain its body temperature. This will disappear before the birth, although a few hairs may remain for a while. A few weeks after that, the baby is covered in vernix, a white, fatty waterproof coating that is thought to protect the now stretching skin from softening in the amniotic fluid. Vernix is the Latin word for 'varnish'.

The baby spends most of its time asleep, roughly divided between 'quiet sleep' and 'active sleep'. It weighs about 2½ lb (1100 g) — about the same as a large bag of sugar. At 28 weeks (seven months) the baby would have a good chance of surviving if born — in medical language it is 'viable'. From now on the baby puts on weight very quickly and positions itself head down, ready to enter the birth canal.

WHAT IS HAPPENING IN YOUR PARTNER'S BODY

The baby is getting heavier and taking up more space. That means your partner's tummy is now heavily swollen, and her back is under quite a lot of strain. By this time she may be putting on weight at a rate of about one pound per week. She may waddle a bit as she walks, and the pressure of the foetus on her lungs and bladder may make her short of breath and in need of frequent visits to the toilet. With your cooking and household skills, you can help ensure this lack of mobility does not affect the running of the home. Her whole body may swell a bit, meaning, for example that she finds rings uncomfortable on her thickening fingers, or that her ankles are swollen.

Her mental state will depend on her attitude to

labour, and how much she enjoyed pregnancy. She may be very relieved the whole business is coming to an end — she has had half a year of not feeling herself — or may be getting really frightened about the birth. If she leaves work during this period (the timing of this varies with each person, and some women work virtually until they give birth) encourage her to enjoy her time.

These last few weeks, especially if the birth is late, can get pretty uncomfortable for her as she manoeuvres her straining bulk about. She may get leg cramps, and constipation. The nausea and fatigue of the early months of pregnancy can return in the last two months.

Some women really object to this phase — but at least it is a sign that the whole process is nearly completed. By about week 36 the baby has moved into position head down into the pelvic cavity ready for birth. This lessons the pressure on the diaphragm and makes breathing easier again — but increases pressure on the bladder, so urinating becomes even more frequent, which can make life pretty monotonous. Earlier in the pregnancy, joints in the pubic area start to loosen in preparation for the stretching they will undergo during labour, and as this slackening progresses this can now cause pain. It may help if your partner uses a walking stick to help her get around. She may not want to, and may only use it in the house, but it will relieve some of the physical strain.

Clearly, from the man's point of view, his partner needs a lot of practical help at this stage. She can't get about easily, she has to go to the loo all the time, and she may be suffering back pain. The demands on you will increase: if you can shop, cook and clean, she will benefit. You may get tired, irritable and resentful. This could reach a peak in the middle of the night if your partner starts to snore. The snoring is caused by an increase in her levels of catarrh, part of a general build up of mucus in her body. You could try gently turning her head to one side as this often clears the passages.

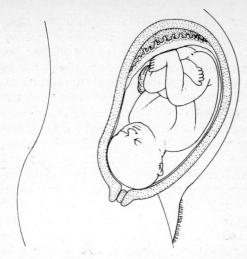

Fig. 4   The foetus at 38 weeks, head down, ready for birth.

ANTE NATAL CLASSES

During these final three months your partner's visits to
the ante natal clinic increase in frequency to fortnightly,
then weekly sessions. Many women find these useful for
the practical guidance and opportunity for exercise they
offer, and the chance to compare notes with other
mothers-to-be. Other women find it a bit of a bore and
get quite tired of the incessant talk about babies. If you
intend to be at the labour, it would be particularly
useful for you to go to some ante natal sessions.

There may be some ante natal classes for men in your
area — your partner will be informed about this.
Sometimes consisting of only one session, these will
include discussion of breathing and relaxation techniques, what happens at the birth (possibly illustrated with
a film), and how to bath and change a baby. Perhaps the
most useful part of the evening will be a chance to chat
with other fathers-to-be.

HELPING YOUR PARTNER

Your partner needs to relax as much as possible during this time. It will build up her energy, relieve any stress she is under, and generally perk her up. You can help by making the conditions right, and talking her gently and softly through each stage.

★ Prepare a soft area such as stacked pillows on a bed, cushions on a sofa or a bean bag on the floor.

★ Get your partner to lie down and make herself comfortable. Later on she may be able to relax sitting down, but it is best to start in this position.

★ She should close her eyes and take long, deep breaths.

★ Talk her through relaxing each part of her body, from toes to scalp, by first tensing, then softening them.

★ Once her body is relaxed, she should simply lie, breathing gently and regularly, for as long as she likes. Keep her away from distractions like a ringing phone or the television.

BREATHING EXERCISES

Your partner needs to learn a number of breathing patterns (psychoprophylaxis), which will help her during the labour. Practising these will help her to relax, feel more ready for the experience, and gives you something useful to do in aiding her. They will also be invaluable to her early in the labour when her contractions start.

If you intend to be at the birth, knowing these

patterns will enable you to remind her of them if she is in pain or forgets them. You should encourage your partner to practise these breathing techniques several times a day. They can sound pretty odd — try them yourself to gain a better understanding of how they feel and to support your partner.

DEEP BREATHING is a major help at the beginning and end of contractions and helps the woman stay calm. She should sit, consciously loosen her body, and breathe deeply and slowly. Air should come in through the nose (the lips should be barely open), out through the mouth, and she should concentrate on filling the bottom of her lungs with air. The breathing should be a gentle, steady rhythm.

CHEST BREATHING also helps cope during the contractions. It is faster, lighter breathing with the air coming into and going out of the mouth. This technique fills only the upper part of the lungs.

HIGH CHEST BREATHING is best for the high point of the contractions and is light breathing with the lips just parted. Occasionally your partner may take in a larger gulp of air, but in the main she will use this very shallow breathing technique.

PANTING helps the woman stop herself pushing the baby too early in the labour (before the cervix has opened up enough). The best technique is to lightly take in and express breath, then give a longer blow — a sort of 'quick quick slow' rhythm. Stay alert for your partner to overwork during these exercises as she may end up hyperventilating (frenetic panting), in which case put your hand in front of her mouth for a short time to restrict the oxygen intake and get her breathing normally again.

HOW ARE YOU FEELING?

Like women, men often have contradictory feelings as the end of pregnancy nears. The rising sense of anticipation and excitement about the starting of a family is balanced by the drudgery of helping your partner get through the day with an increasingly cumbersome and uncooperative body.

Fears about deformity in the baby can build up now, but you can console yourself with the thought that 97 percent of babies born are completely 'normal'. The remaining 3 percent are equally split: those whose damage can be repaired; those with physical deformities, and those with a mental handicap. A healthy mum who received good care throughout her pregnancy is very unlikely to produce an abnormal baby unless there is a hereditary fault or if she is nearer 40 than 30. It is also only fair to point out that many handicapped babies are loved by their parents as much as if they were 'normal' — but no-one would deny that some major adjustments are necessary.

PRACTICAL HELP

You may feel powerless to do much more than offer support during this period, but there are many practical steps you can take.

1. As the pregnancy nears an end, remind your employer that you may want to take some time off at quite short notice. This applies whether or not you intend to be at the birth. You and your partner will still want some time together at home as a family even if you were not in the delivery room.
2. Start looking at any danger points in the house that

could cause trouble to someone carrying a baby. These may include:

● Trailing electrical leads which could trip her up.
● Mats which move about on the floor and could cause her to slip.
● Uneven steps.
● Shiny, slippery floors.
● Bits of furniture which jut out. Carrying a baby about reduces your field of vision and your agility. You will find bruises to show for any objects which block her path!
● Low hanging lights which you have become adept at swaying to avoid.

3. Towards the end of the pregnancy, your partner will be advised to prepare a case with everything she may need at the hospital both for herself and for the baby.

4. You may find it useful to prepare your own bag of things that you or your partner may find useful if you plan to be with her for the birth. This might include:

● Personal stereo and tapes.
● Something to spray a fine mist of refreshing water on your partner (plant spray bottles are good).
● A sponge to wipe your partner's face.
● Lipsalve to prevent her lips becoming chapped.
● Toiletries, including shaving materials — you could be there for a while.
● A camera to take a photo of your partner with the new baby. Put in a high-speed film as you do not want to use a flash.
● Chocolate and other provisions — you might well miss a meal at home or the hospital.

There will be other items you will wish to take in (flowers, fruit, sandwiches) which cannot be prepared in advance. Put a note of them on top of the bag so that you don't forget them.

5. It is a good idea to prepare a card listing all the useful telephone numbers you will need when the labour starts: the GP, the midwife, the hospital, the taxi firm, etc.
6. Do a dry run of the journey to the hospital. Time it. Work out an alternative route.
7. Keep your car well maintained and, in particular, with enough petrol for the journey to the hospital and back.
8. Stock up on food. While your wife is in hospital you will want to visit her much of the time, so pile the freezer up with meals you can just heat up when you need to.

SEX DURING PREGNANCY

There is still no physical reason why you cannot both enjoy making love throughout this period — although there may be mental blocks about it and certain positions which are uncomfortable. If your partner has an orgasm, it may set off contractions of muscles in the womb. These are called Braxton Hicks contractions and are harmless (if a little alarming the first time): they do not signal the start of labour. She should lie quietly and let them pass.

PREPARING THE HOME

You will have opportunities later on to give the home a freshen up with flowers and a quick hoover before your partner returns. However, towards the end of the pregnancy it is worth getting in the following materials and equipment. You will probably not have to buy all this, certainly not new: friends and relatives are often very generous in what they are prepared to provide, and if some have already had children, they may be able to loan or give you equipment. Borrowing or buying second-hand is prudent and saves you money to buy really useful, long-term things for your child.

By the time the new baby is ready to be brought home you will need:

1. Moses basket, useful for first 4–6 months for baby to sleep in or for you to carry baby around. Can be placed in carry cot when travelling by car. Secure carry cot with safety straps.
2. Cot, for when it outgrows the basket.
3. Sheets for the cot (you could cut up old ones, or use a pillow case).
4. Blanket for cot.
5. Baby wipes.
6. Nappies. Disposable nappies are one of the great modern boons for parents. Towelling (thick cotton) washable nappies are often considered better for the night as they are more absorbent. You need a hefty supply of disposables — otherwise you can guarantee you will run out halfway on a journey in the middle of nowhere!
7. Baby clothes. Your partner (or indeed you) may already be knitting furiously. Friends and relatives may make, loan or give clothes. Don't go mad buying them, as the baby grows out of them very quickly.
8. Plastic pants.
9. Changing mat.
10. Sponge or face cloth.
11. Soft towels to dry the baby.
12. Baby lotion and oil, petroleum jelly.
13. Blunt-ended scissors for cutting nails.
14. Cotton wool buds.

Chapter 5

THE BIRTH

Whether or not you intend to be at the birth, you will find this chapter useful. It will brief you on what happens throughout your partner's labour, and how you can help, both at the time and afterwards. I have included and explained a number of technical terms as they are likely to be used by the hospital staff and you will feel happier if you understand what they are talking about.

Today labour is rather different and men are more involved, and can offer a lot more support to their partners. Some of them may pretend not to like this, but in reality, the beginning of modern fatherhood is a good deal more satisfying than being left out at this important time.

There are three stages to labour.

1. Contractions, a series of muscle spasms, start to open up the cervix at the base of the womb. The contractions can go on for many hours before you need to head for the hospital.
2. When the cervix is open wide enough for the baby to exit, the contractions combine with your partner's pushing to ease the baby out.
3. The placenta, the wall of the womb which has been the channel of nourishment for the foetus (via the umbilical cord), is released.

How labour begins
There are three possible signs that labour is

beginning. If you want to be with your wife during labour and are away when these things happen, make sure she has a telephone number where she can contact you. If you are staying at work for a while, it is best if you call her every half hour so that you know how things are progressing.

- A show. The mucus plug sealing the womb becomes dislodged and exits via the vagina. This is not a sign to charge to the hospital, but always precedes the next stage, rupture of the membranes.
- Breaking of the waters. The foetus has been cosily cocooned inside the amniotic sac. In effect, the bag ruptures, releasing amniotic fluid (which is a clear, straw colour). Water will start running down your partner's legs, which could make life complicated if you are in the supermarket! You should phone the hospital or your midwife. If they have not started already contractions are likely to start within 24 hours.
- Contractions. These are tightening of muscles in the abdomen, which then relax again.

THE FIRST STAGE OF LABOUR

The first contractions are quite mild for most women, and may occur regularly but then stop altogether. Your partner should have been will briefed on this at her ante natal clinic. Such contractions are a signal of the commencement of labour, but there is no need to do anything. Your partner will be most comfortable moving slowly about. You can chat, carry on with everyday life — whatever relaxes her most. Your partner is likely to start giving birth within 24 hours — the average for a first baby is 12–14 hours — so the less fatigued she gets now, the better.

A warm bath may soothe her, but keeping occupied will help her avoid getting obsessed with the contractions and simply waiting for the next one, which will make her anxious. She is probably better off not lying in bed, as this will give her less to do and carries a message of illness. Many couples find this calm period before the turmoil of giving birth is one of the most enjoyable parts of the labour.

You or your partner should be keeping a note of the intervals between contractions. When they get stronger and become regular at (usually) every 10–15 minutes it is time to go to the hospital. Phone them first to allow time to prepare for admission. If you are going by car, your partner will be most comfortable finding her own position on the back seat, rather than being strapped in the front. Keep calm, there is no need to hurry the journey. If you do not have a car, you may need to call a taxi or, if you are concerned there may be a medical problem, an ambulance. Don't forget to bring both your bags (see previous chapter for checklist) and add the fresh items such as sandwiches and fruit, because you may miss meal times at the hospital.

PAIN

Before we describe your role in the process of labour, it is worth making a few points about pain. Most women experience considerable pain during childbirth, especially for the first birth. However, the breathing you have practised with your partner can be a major help by taking her mind off the sensation and controlling her contractions. Furthermore, some women speak of experiencing a peculiar exhilaration during labour, a 'high'. This is partly a mental phenomenon linked to the joy of bringing life, and partly a physical reaction as the body produces certain painkilling chemicals.

That said, we all have our limits, and if your partner is in too much pain there are drugs which can help (see pages 54–55). You should have discussed what drugs she was prepared to have over the last few weeks, and will now be able to ask for them if she is not able to. However much a woman wants a 'natural' (drug free) birth, there is no point turning herself into a martyr if she is in pain.

YOUR ROLE

Your role at the labour is to support your partner, by talking to her, praising her, making sure she is comfortable and interpreting her needs: basically doing all you can to make the labour pleasurable. You can remind her about her breathing techniques and listen and watch to make sure she is not breathing too vigorously, which can lead to hyperventilation. That said, she may find someone talking to her distracting and irritating, so be sensitive to her needs, and insensitive about critical comments she makes to you — she needs you there, not sulking next door. You can also help alleviate abdominal pain by applying a strong massage towards the base of her spine. If your partner is on her side, you will be able to do this standing behind her. Otherwise you could kneel in front of her and put your arms over her head so that you can massage the back with your hands. You will need stamina to keep doing this, as a gentle rubbing is no good: it must be done with some pressure.

One point to remember throughout labour is the importance of looking at your partner in the eyes as much as possible. Avoiding eye contact is a sub-conscious sign of concern which your partner will detect, and she needs reassurance and support, not anxiety signals.

People have different ways of coping with stress, and it is very common for partners to become quite abusive as the contractions get stronger and more painful. Be prepared to hear some pretty strong language being directed at you. Many men are astonished at this aspect of the labour, but verbal aggression can be highly therapeutic. It is also worth reminding her that the more painful the contractions, the more they are likely to achieve — so the nearer you are to the birth.

AT THE HOSPITAL

When you get to the hospital you will need to book in at the admissions desk before your partner is examined by a midwife. She will make a number of checks including how far the cervix has dilated. You will also see the anaesthetist if you have requested pain relief. Your partner will not need to enter the delivery room and push the baby out until the cervix is wide enough (approximately 10 cm) for the baby. You may be left together for quite some time, waiting for the contractions to get the body right for the next stage. Your partner should not start trying to push the baby out without consulting the midwife, even if her body starts giving signals to do so. This is because the top of the cervix may dilate enough to allow the baby's head to fall (and set off the 'push' stimulus), but if the lower part of the cervix is still not open enough birth cannot take place. Dilation gets progressively faster, so the first 5 cm take longer than the second half of the process. Dilation is always referred to in centimetres.

Your partner may be given an enema in which her bowels are emptied, via the rectum, with warm soapy water. Undignified, yes, but it supposedly leaves more room for the baby and saves the embarrassment of going while pushing during labour. Also pretty undigni-

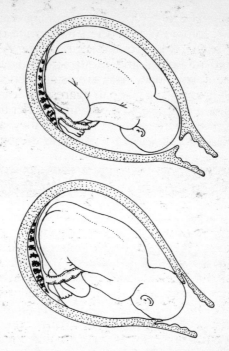

Fig. 5   The cervix dilates to allow the baby's head through, followed by its body.

fied is the gown and overshoes you may be given to wear at the labour. Incidentally you should be wearing loose, comfortable clothes — hospitals are kept very warm and you could be there some time. A change of shoes may be welcome.

The baby's position will have been checked at the ante natal visits to judge if there are any likely problems, and this is repeated at the start of labour. Head up or head down is known as a longitudinal lie. Lying across the womb is called a transverse or oblique lie, and a Caesarean will probably be performed (see page 59). The 'presentation' of the baby indicates which part of it will come out first. Head downwards is called cephalic or vertex presentation, and makes for the easiest birth as the head is the largest part of the baby's body. Thankfully 96 percent of babies are like this. The rest are in a breech presentation when the bottom or feet are facing down. If this could not be corrected during the pregnancy, birth will be slightly more difficult, but may well still be via the vagina, with more help from staff through an episiotomy and forceps (see pages 58–59). Otherwise a Caesarean will be necessary.

Labour will be made easier if the baby is facing towards your partner's backbone (an anterior position), but if it is the other way round (a posterior position) the process is slowed down a little.

PAIN RELIEF

Your partner may now be in a lot of pain. If it is getting too much for her, she may say so, or you may be able to tell from her expression. Pain relief is available in the following forms:

GAS: Entonox is a blend of oxygen and nitrous oxide which your partner breathes in through a mask. It takes the edge off pain and can induce a slight feeling of light-headedness.

INJECTIONS: A drug, usually pethidine, is administered and takes about 20 minutes to start relieving the pain. It can cause drowsiness in mother and/or the baby.

EPIDURAL: An epidural is a local anaesthetic which removes all sensation from the birth canal, and usually causes numbness through the lower half of the body. Not all hospitals can offer it and **it may need to be booked in advance** (it requires an anaesthetist). Your partner will be put on a drip feed and the anaesthetic will be applied via a needle and tube to the lower back. An epidural may be used to help a woman in severe pain who is having a difficult birth. It tends to turn the labour into a medical exercise, because a lot of monitoring of mother and baby is required. It may be distressing for you to see your partner being treated like an accident victim with drips and injections, but of course the main thing is that she is free of pain and can deliver the baby.

TENS: This stands for 'transcutaneous electrical nerve stimulation', and involves four electrodes placed on the lower back which encourage the body to produce its own painkillers (endorphins) and to block pain sensation with an electric current. Your partner is able to control the amount of current administered herself. This method of pain control is not always successful with strong labour pains.

THE SECOND STAGE OF LABOUR

Once dilation is complete and the cervix is about 10 cm wide, chances are the baby will be born within an hour. Now, instead of simply breathing through each contraction and allowing the cervix to dilate, your partner also has a physical role in pushing the baby out. She will probably have decided in advance which position she would like to be in. Lying spread out on a bed is not necessarily the best position from which to give birth. Other positions include:

1. Squatting on the haunches.
2. Kneeling.
3. Squatting on all fours.

Your partner may have opted for an 'active birth'. This is basically an attempt to give birth in the most natural way, with full freedom of movement and no drugs if possible. Sometimes this simply involves trying several positions, but she may have decided to ask for a water birth (in which she is put into an upright bath) or a birthing stool. You will have discussed her preferences and your role in advance (see birth plan, page 31). She may want you to support her back as she squats, or just to hold her hand and mop her brow. If you are supporting her, get as comfortable as possible: you could be there for some time without being able to move again. Try to arrange some support for your body, from a wall, for example.

The contractions which expel the baby should be long and powerful. Each does a little bit to move the child nearer the opening. Eventually the head appears. Although you may have seen photographs of this stage of birth taken from feet level, your view will be very different. Sheets often cover the midriff and if you are holding your partner's head, for example, you may not be able to see the baby appear unless you make a special effort. Some hospitals offer a strategically placed mirror so you can both see the baby emerging. However it is useful if you can report progress to her between wiping her face with a refreshing cloth between contractions and generally offering encouragement.

There may be various items of high-tech equipment in the delivery room, including a machine to monitor the baby's heartbeat, and another which indicates when the contractions are about to start. This second machine can help you to warn your partner to prepare for the next contraction, which she will find very useful. The heartbeat machine is fascinating, but some fathers find they become pre-occupied with watching it and may be distracted from supporting their partners.

Once the head is delivered the rest of the baby's body follows relatively easily, because the head is disproportionately large. The baby will still be attached to the placenta by the umbilical cord, which is pegged and then cut (it is not nerve tissue so this is painless even though it may still be pulsating). The time when you and your partner meet your child for the first time is a precious one, never to be repeated, and you may become quite emotional — perhaps to your own surprise. The relief after the strain of watching your partner cope with labour, the onset of tiredness as your body stops calling up its reserves of energy, and the pleasure of seeing your child can combine to make the toughest man cry. Other men may feel quite unmoved about it all and see the labour almost as if in a dream — there is no set rule about your reactions, but remember to embrace and congratulate your partner too — she worked harder than you did for this moment! In the meantime the doctor will make a few checks on the baby including some which produce the APGAR score on Appearance, Pulse, Grimace (reflex) Activity and Respiration. This system is a measurement (marked from 0 to 2) of the extent, if any, of lack of oxygen in a newborn baby.

THE THIRD STAGE OF LABOUR

The delivery of the placenta, the womb lining which housed the baby, is usually quickened with an injection of a drug called synotemetrine into the thigh. This reduces the risk of your partner losing too much blood. If your partner prefers not to have drugs, it should take up to 20 minutes to release the placenta, which looks like liver and is checked to ensure no remnants are left in the womb. After the birth, in addition to wanting to hold her baby, she may well be hungry after her exertions, so your supply of nuts and raisins, chocolate, and other food may be appreciated.

LEBOYER BIRTH

During the pregnancy you may hear references to a 'Leboyer birth'. Frederick Leboyer is a French doctor who recommends that birth should be trauma-free for the baby and the mother. Among the things he suggests are:

★ Subdued lighting — the baby has been in darkness until now.
★ Soft, welcoming sounds.
★ Not cutting the umbilical cord until it stops pulsating.
★ Placing the baby in warm water to replicate conditions in the womb after it has been laid on the mother's tummy for a while.

Your partner may opt for all or some of the elements of a Leboyer birth in her birth plan.

MEDICAL HELP FOR BIRTH

FORCEPS OR VACUUM BIRTH

Forceps are large, specially designed tongs which help the baby out. They are used to hurry the birth if the baby or mother is in danger or if the contractions are not strong enough to push it out. The process is pretty undignified: your partner's legs are put into stirrups and she is given a local anaesthetic and episiotomy. The tongs grip the baby's head and gently ease it out. If staff suggest the use of forceps, ask them why it is necessary. Your partner has every right to refuse if there is no urgent medical reason to use them. An alternative to the forceps is a vacuum extraction (ventouse delivery) in which a small cap is attached to the baby's head and suction is used to help the birth.

EPISIOTOMY

This is a cut from the vaginal opening towards the anus, to widen the gap for the baby to exit through. It may be necessary if the baby is found to be at an angle, or is tearing the tissue in your partner's vagina. It is always used for a forceps or vacuum delivery. Stirrups and an anaesthetic are used, and after the birth the cut is carefully stitched back up to keep the muscle and skin separate. You may find it distressing to see the cut being made, in which case don't look!

CAESARIAN BIRTH

A Caesarian is when the baby is removed from the womb through a cut made in your partner's lower abdomen. Obviously this is necessary only if it cannot be born by exiting down the vagina. About 15 percent of European births are by this method — slightly more in the USA. Chances are the operation will be planned in advance because some problem such as the foetus's position is spotted, so you will be able to prepare yourselves in advance. If you want to be present, say so. Your partner will have a local anaesthetic (epidural) and will be screened from seeing the operation by sheets. Her pubic hair will be shaved and the incision made in this area. If for some reason the Caesarian becomes a necessity during a normal birth, there will be no time for an epidural to take effect and your partner will be given a general anaesthetic. The baby will be taken out within a few minutes, but it will take at least half an hour to stitch up the wound. This is a major operation and your partner will probably take a month at least to fully recover — especially after a general anaesthetic. She will be so tired and incapable of movement that even reaching over to hold the baby in the ward may be impossible. You can help by handing her the baby, holding it yourself and reporting on its movements. Caesarian can be traumatic because what should be a happy birth becomes major surgery. You may both benefit from some specialist counselling to cope with the sense of disappointment such a birth can cause.

PREMATURE BIRTH

As has been stated on page 18, the 'due date' of a baby is only an approximate day, and there is nothing unusual about reaching labour a couple of weeks early. However, 7 percent of babies are born before the 37th week of pregnancy and this is classified as premature birth. Sometimes early labour is induced to protect the mother, or is brought on because there are two foetuses in the womb (which would probably have been apparent from the scan, and happens in one out of every 276 pregnancies). If the birth is not induced and you are not expecting twins, early labour will be a shock for both of you. Your partner is bound to be anxious, and you may feel concerned and under-prepared too. Phone the hospital immediately. If you are away from home, try the nearest hospital with a maternity unit.

There can be a few problems during premature labour, but the hospital staff will be experienced in handling the situation. Your partner will need your support more than ever: she may be frightened and unsure what is happening. Don't be afraid to ask staff what is going on, and what she should be doing. If she needs you to, act as her interpreter and keep her informed. Once born, premature babies are kept in a warm environment such as an incubator. This can be traumatic as your partner will have very little contact with her child, and you will see it in a temperature controlled capsule surrounded by leads and monitors. Check on your child frequently and report back to your partner. Take a polaroid photograph of the baby for her — she may like to keep it by her bedside. Naturally you will be concerned, but premature babies have an excellent survival rate in hospitals (more than 95 per cent if born after 35 weeks, 90 percent if between 27 and 29 weeks).

SLOW OR LATE LABOUR

If the labour is taking a long time, or is overdue, an induced birth may be suggested. If you are still at home, waiting for everything to start, talk it over with the midwife, doctor or consultant. Do not allow the hospital staff to place unnecessary pressure on you to agree just for conveniences sake! Ask them to explain the benefits and disadvantages of induction in this case. Clearly, if inducing birth will stop your partner suffering, or prevent damage to her or the baby, you will both want to go ahead. Labour can be started by inserting pessaries in the vagina, by artificially breaking the waters, or feed synthetic hormones through a drip.

STILL BIRTH

The very idea of going through labour to produce a baby that is dead is nightmarish. It happens in about 0.15 percent of births, and is usually caused by a fault in the placenta, although very small or severely handicapped babies can be stillborn. You and your partner would almost certainly benefit from counselling to cope with this traumatic event.

EMERGENCY BIRTH

- **Call for an ambulance**, tell your partner to pant to help her stop pushing the baby out.
- Ensure your partner is comfortable and supported with cushions.
- Put down newspapers or plastic sheets (bin bags or a shower curtain) where she will deliver.
- Wash your hands and forearms with soap and water to avoid infection. Use antiseptic in the water if possible.
- As the birth progresses, the baby's head will appear. Do not pull it, but check that the umbilical cord is not around its neck as it will choke. If it is, push the head in a little and gently move the cord around it (it is quite flexible). When the head is out, clear mucus from the mouth and nose to help the baby breathe.
- Move the head around a little to help the rest of the body ease out of the birth canal. Keep your partner informed and ask her to push when the time is right.
- Following birth, wrap it in a clean towel or blanket. It must be kept warm. Do not tug the umbilical cord. When the placenta follows, keep it in a container as it needs to be checked to make sure none is left in the womb. Keep it higher than the baby so that blood does not flow from the child into the placenta.
- If the baby is not breathing, pinch, rub and slap it to stimulate it. It this does not work, suck the nose gently to clear the passages, otherwise blow softly into the nose, pause, and repeat.
- Keep the mother and baby warm. By this time the doctor or an ambulance will have arrived.

AFTER THE BIRTH

Most babies cry soon after the birth. This is a good sign — it shows the lungs are working properly, something that does not happen automatically as the baby has not needed to work them before. The midwife will check this, and remove any blockages in the mouth or nostrils that can hinder breathing. She may hold the baby upside down to encourage the lungs to work properly. Soon after birth, most babies are surprisingly alert. They will stare wide-eyed at the nearest person and may even interact with whoever is holding them by doing things like poking their tongues out. It is assumed that this is part of the 'bonding' process when parent and baby get to know each other. After a couple of hours this energy and curiosity seems to evaporate and the baby turns into a sleeping/feeding doll.

WHAT A BABY LOOKS LIKE

Most babies weigh between 6 and 8 pounds (about 3 kilos). Your first instinct is likely to be to look to see if you have a boy or a girl, then check it has the right number of toes and fingers. At first sight, babies hardly look human at all. For the first few minutes they are blue (until the circulation gets going) and in the case of dark-skinned babies, rather grey. They may be a bit bruised, covered in blood (from breaks in your partner's vaginal tissue), and have streaks of a white substance (the vernix which appeared as a protective covering around week 28). The bones are soft and the head may have become misshapen during the birth, especially if forceps were used. The skull takes on a more natural shape after a few hours. Babies born by Caesarian section look a lot healthier because they have not been crammed into a tight space to leave the womb.

The child (which will undoubtedly appear to father and mother as the most beautiful baby in the world) may also have:

1. Swollen genitals, which will reduce in size.
2. Fine downy body hair, the lanugo, which will fall out.
3. A squint (which should self-correct within six months, otherwise consult your doctor).
4. Jaundice, a yellowing of the skin which is caused by a blood problem and is usually corrected by the liver although some treatment may be necessary.
5. Your child may have, or develop over the next few days, a birthmark. This can be upsetting and you will be worried that the mark is permanent. It rarely is.

From that list it is clear that you may feel some sense of alarm or concern when you first see your baby. After nine months, you were hoping to be presented with a bonny baby, and instead you have a misshapen, oddly coloured being. Rest assured that it will look more like the advertiser's idea of a baby in a matter of hours. Your partner may be sharing your sense of disappointment, but it is probably better to make positive statements and hide your concern, or at least refer to any seeming imperfections in a light-hearted way. Women are very good at attaching blame to themselves, and it would be awful if your partner ended her labour feeling guilty about something she had no control over.

That said, you probably will not mind any little blemishes on your new child: every parent in the world will tell you how beautiful their own baby was at birth, and how they felt sorry for the other parents because their newborn children were so wrinkled! You will be tired now (but not as worn out as your partner) so give yourself some time for peace and quiet with your new family. Depending on the time of day, you may be able to get something to eat for yourself and your partner, or raid your 'emergency rations'. Many fathers report that a cup of lukewarm water tasted as good as champagne at this time.

BIRTH RIGHTS

It is important to know what your rights are when it comes to having a baby. Your partner may feel emotional or in pain when it is time to make a decision and it will help if you can act as spokesman.

★ Your partner does not need to have her pubic hair shaved before the birth, unless she is having a Caesarian delivery.

★ She does not have to agree to an enema, unless constipated.

★ She does not have to agree to a routine episiotomy for a quicker birth. She may choose a longer delivery time as long as this will not endanger the health of the baby.

★ She does not have to accept any drugs without discussion beforehand.

★ Your partner may request breast feeding on demand for the days spent in hospital after the birth.

Chapter 6

THE VISITING FATHER

After the birth, your partner's life revolves around feeding and caring for her baby in hospital for a few days until staff are content neither would be at risk at home. The father's status drops from labour companion to visitor, and he can only visit his partner during certain periods, and must go home to feed himself and sleep. Many men find this is a strange transition which leaves them feeling in limbo.

You will probably carry on working until the baby is due to come home, and by now you will have some idea from the doctors when this is likely to be. You should already have some leave booked, but should probably confirm this with your employer. If your wife has undergone a Caesarian she will definitely need help and you may want to take more time off than you had planned. Talk to your employer — you may be able to take a couple of days sick leave.

So, at a time when you have become a father, and have shared in the experience of labour, you are suddenly on your own. It can feel odd. You may bore people stupid with descriptions of your child because you have no one else to tell. The spare time when you might have gone to see friends will probably be spent travelling to and from the hospital. You will want to telephone close relatives to give them the happy news. They are bound to want to know your baby's sex and weight, the time of birth, the length of labour, who it looks like, the mother's health — but not how you are coping with your strange half-life and what your feelings are. You may find that you feel powerless and even a bit depressed. It may help to stay with friends or relatives at this time instead of the empty house which you identify so much with your life with your partner.

VISITING YOUR NEW FAMILY

You will need to discuss your feelings with your partner. That is not easy in hospital. You can only visit at certain times, there are other people nearby, and sometimes there are other visitors talking to your partner. It is best to set aside some visiting time when you and your partner can be alone, or just have the baby for company. Tell any prospective visitors that they are very welcome during standard visiting hours except, say, 6–7 p.m. That can be the period when you arrive from work and have a chance to be with each other. Some men say visiting their partner in hospital after the birth is like meeting a stranger: the circumstances are new and can be difficult, she is probably tired and a little worried at times; you are tired too, and face the prospect of an empty home to go back to. This time can be more stressful than anything you experienced during the birth!

REGISTERING THE BIRTH

By law you must register the birth of the baby within 42 days of its birth (21 days for Scotland). If the birth was in a hospital, your partner will probably be visited by the registrar of births, so the job can be done on the spot. Otherwise you may need to go to the Registry Office. Either way the procedure is very simple — the hardest part of it is agreeing on the name!

GETTING TO KNOW YOUR BABY

Parents are expected to feel love for their offspring. You will too — but not necessarily yet. You may have a massive surge of emotion from the moment the baby appears, and love it from then on. But there are fathers and mothers who need time to adjust before they feel this love. You may simply feel unsettled, unsure about how you are both going to cope with a baby, about the changes imposed on your life — all the doubts you had during the pregnancy will not automatically evaporate after the birth.

You have a lot of learning to do in handling your baby. Mothers get lots of advice and practice, and all their time is devoted to their child in its first few days. For dads it is different. You don't see your new family as often as you might like, and when you do you can't chat properly with your partner because of the hospital setting and the demanding presence of the baby. Women (not usually your partner) can be very odd when you handle the baby. First, they offer comments on how well (or, more often badly) you are holding the baby. They invite you to talk to it — the surest thing to empty your mind of coherent thought. In fact, ironically enough, some women are just plain unhelpful. This belittling behaviour is called 'matronising', and some feminists might see it as revenge for men's attitudes to women the rest of the time! Given a little practice you will be confidently picking up your baby, providing a comfortable support for its weak neck, looking into its eyes, and sensing that special kind of communication that parents have with their babies.

Everybody knows that babies cannot understand human speech. Yet we will all talk to a baby as we hold it or lean over it in its cot. This is a natural instinct and helps the baby in the long term in learning to talk, which it will do by mimicking voices it hears. But what we say to babies is not for their benefit: it is dictated by the other people in the room. It takes time to get used to talking to a baby in front of other people. You feel self-conscious and say silly things to try to be funny or impress them. Then you feel bad about saying things for their benefit and not for the baby — even though it can't understand what you are saying! After a few sessions you will get used to it.

HOLDING A BABY

Babies love skin contact and holding your child can be a wonderful experience in itself. But the first time you pick up a baby you will probably be terrified — it rarely comes naturally to men. Ironically, men's larger hands make them well-suited to holding a baby properly, as they provide the necessary support. Babies have heavy heads and under-developed necks. So they cannot support the head properly: you have to do it for them. You can practise anytime by putting the little finger edge of your outstretched hand against your midriff, and pushing your elbow out. That is the position in which the baby will be most secure and comfortable — and it can feel your heartbeat through your chest. When you are more confident you may put the baby upright up your chest, its head resting on your shoulder — but keep your hand ready to support it if necessary.

FEEDING

Your partner will have chosen whether she wants to breast feed the baby, and if she chose to she will be learning the intricacies of this process. The milk the baby receives in the first few days is called colostrum and is more of a 'milk'-looking liquid. After this, breast milk looks thinner. The baby sucks milk from the nipples, which as a result can become sore and cracked. As demand for milk rises or falls, so the woman's body responds. If the baby is a hungry one, your partner's breasts will get very full and may leak a bit. Your partner should insist on her right to feed the baby on demand while she is in the hospital.

The more contact you have with the baby, the more relaxed and confident you will feel about handling it, and it would seem about fatherhood as a whole. The most common comment I have heard from first time fathers is 'I needn't have worried so much — and I didn't think I would enjoy having a baby around so much.'

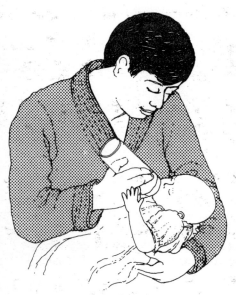

Fig. 6 A comfortable position for bottle feeding.

Chapter 7

THE HOMECOMING

It is a special moment when your partner is ready to come home and brings in the baby for the first time. You may find yourself showing it around the house like a prospective purchaser! Do what you like — it is part of the enjoyment of parenthood.

PREPARING FOR THE HOMECOMING

Now is the time to check that you have everything you need to cope with the baby. Go through the list on page 47 as a check. Your partner will appreciate you going to the trouble of tidying up the home, even if it means you paid someone else to come and do it! Flowers brighten up rooms and are a very expressive gesture.

There are a number of practical steps you can take to ensure the safety of your baby over the coming months. Even if they cannot walk, after about six months some babies can roll or crawl about, and once they are mobile you must make sure the home is safe for them, because they have no idea of what is dangerous.

★ Fit a gate at the top of stairs.
★ Check that stair carpet is properly fixed.
★ Put fireguards on all electric, gas and open fires.
★ Put safety covers into all plugs when not in use.

★ Wherever glass is at a low level or near where the baby will crawl, fit safety glass or apply safety film.

★ Buy a pram net to keep out cats.

★ Fit a cooker guard, and train yourself to turn all saucepan handles inwards, away from the edge of the oven. Use the back burners whenever possible.

★ Get into the habit of always emptying the kettle after use.

★ Get rid of any unused fridges or freezers a toddler could climb into.

★ Buy or make a playpen and check it has no sharp edges and cannot collapse.

★ Move all medicines, drugs and dangerous chemicals to a safe height (preferably out of eyesight) and label them clearly. Dangerous household chemicals include cleaning materials, hairspray and weedkiller.

★ Keep all plastic bags in one drawer out of reach. Get into the habit of knotting these items so that even if the baby does get hold of them it cannot pull them over its head and suffocate.

★ Remove all locks at toddler height (they could lock themselves in a room by accident and not be able to get out) — use latch fittings higher up. Make sure no toddler could open the front or back door unaided.

★ Check that all toys are non-toxic and have no sharp edges or small pieces that could be put in a mouth and choked on.

The concept of paternity leave (giving fathers time off to be with their new children) is accepted in some countries, and derided in others. It is very important that you do make the effort to get at least several days off to be at home. If you cannot, your partner will certainly appreciate help from other people, and perhaps her mother or a sister or friend will be able to come and stay.

Some men like to give their partners a present when

they come home — a necklace or ring, perhaps, and definitely for her and nothing to do with the baby — but do not feel obliged to do this. Do, however, try to 'woo' your partner a little to show that you are welcoming her home as well as the baby. At this time, and for the next few months, many men are reduced to astonished admiration at their partners for handling the labour and coping with the demands of the baby with apparent ease. Oddly, this can make the man quite passive and reserved. This is probably tied up with the fact that the partner has become a mother, and we start to see her in a mother's, rather than a lover's role. Be prepared for these feelings and for adjusting to them.

VISITORS

Everyone will want to meet your new baby, particularly its grandparents. Your partner's mother or some other relative may have been invited to come and help out in the house in these early days. Or you may have chosen to keep this as a time for yourselves alone to share with the baby. Either way, family, friends and well-wishers are bound to telephone and perhaps call round to see the baby. This can cause some difficulties.

If someone arrives at the door and your partner is asleep, or too tired to see anyone, explain this tactfully and suggest they call back in a few days, or that you will telephone to say when a visit would be worthwhile. You may wish to give them a cup of tea and update them on the news, indeed it may be very good for you to share your feelings with someone else. Discuss with your partner who she is happy to see anytime and who she would prefer you to 'put off' for now. Bear in mind that she may feel low at times and want the support and reassurance of her friends and relations — there may be people she *wants* to be woken up to see.

Family visitors and others who you know your partner would want to see should be warned that she is tired and they would be best advised to make short, frequent visits rather than expect to spend an afternoon chatting. Obviously you will want to be diplomatic about this but you will be under strain so be prepared for the occasional outburst! It is always better to agree to visits over the telephone so that you have controllable numbers at convenient times.

CRYING

Nothing can make a parent feel as hopeless as a crying baby. It is a piercing and haunting noise that acts like an alarm signal. Men often feel worse about this than women, because a man cannot offer a comforting milk-filled breast to a wailing baby. The problem is not always hunger, however. Babies may cry because they are uncomfortable (check the nappy, are they too hot or cold, is there bright light shining into their eyes?), tired (gently rocking them, or just leaving them alone can bring sleep), or just want a bit of attention. You will be surprised at how you learn what is the best action to take.

You may find offering the baby a dummy helps. As with many aspects of parenthood, the use of the dummy is the subject of much debate. Some people say it can distort the growth of their teeth, confuse them by replicating the nipple without supplying food, and create a problem because sometime the child must be weaned off the dummy. Others argue that it comforts the child and does no damage. The baby may settle the dilemma by sucking its thumb.

BOTTLE FEEDING

If and when you feed the baby from a bottle, check with your partner whether the baby likes its drink warmed or is content with it cold. You will need to sterilise all the equipment you are using to prevent the baby catching an infection.

HOW TO STERILISE EQUIPMENT

With chemicals

1. Using fresh washing up water, give the bottles and teats a thorough wash, squeezing water through the teat, and rinse in clean water.
2. Immerse the equipment in the made-up sterilising solution in a lidded container. Make sure there are no air bubbles in the bottles, and that everything is submerged below the surface. Leave for the stipulated length of time.
3. Boil a kettle and allow this water to cool. Use this, and not tap water, to give the equipment a final rinse after removing it from the chemical solution.
4. Change sterilising fluid after 24 hours.

With boiling water

1. Wash everything thoroughly as above.
2. Put everything in a large saucepan with plenty of water (check there are no air bubbles) and boil it for at least ten minutes.
3. Drain the pan but keep the bottles and teats in it with the lid on until they are needed.

How to bottle feed

1. Wash your hands.
2. Once the made-up or expressed milk is in the bottle give it a good shake. Breast milk in particular tends to separate after a while.
3. If the feed is to be warmed (after all, breast milk is warm) stand the bottle in a jug of hot water. Check it does not get too hot by squirting a little onto your wrist to test the temperature.
4. Get into a comfortable position which you can stay in for a while. Feeding can take a long time, and the baby may fall asleep for a while. Settle yourself on some cushions in front of the TV!
5. Make sure the baby is settled and has some contact with your skin.
6. Put the teat very close to the baby's mouth, as the baby is not mobile enough to move towards it. You may need to show it the teat and stroke it on the baby's cheek to encourage it to feed.
7. Keep the bottle tipped up so that there is always milk in the teat — otherwise your baby may be sucking in air which will not do it any good. The teat may get flattened so check it every so often, and pull the bottle back slightly to allow the teat to refill.
8. NEVER leave a baby to feed unattended, perhaps by propping up the bottle — it could choke.
9. Vigorous sucking may produce a vacuum which will cause the teat to collapse, so pull the bottle back slightly every so often to allow the teat to resume its shape.
10. When your baby refuses any more (give it a chance to change its mind first) throw away the left-over milk.
11. After the feed, pat or rub the baby's back (it might be easiest if you put it on your shoulder) to get it to burp out any wind.

CHANGING A NAPPY

Babies get through something like 2,000 nappies in a year. That is a lot of nappy changing! The introduction of disposable nappies freed many homes from the smelly and time-consuming duty of washing out towelling nappies. Most parents agree the higher cost of paying for disposables is well worth it. However towelling nappies are still very much in use too, sometimes as night nappies because they are more absorbent than the modern kind. Some men claim they never change their babies, as if this is some mark of achievement or masculinity. In fact, it is a sign of selfishness, because changing a nappy is as much a duty for both parents as providing toys and warmth. Nobody can pretend that changing a nappy is a pleasant experience, but it has to be done, and the job should be shared.

CHANGING A NAPPY

You will need:

★ Changing mat (optional but very useful and doubles as a play mat for the baby — otherwise use a towel with plastic sheet on top).
★ Cotton wool and tissues.
★ Baby lotion or cream.
★ Soap and water.
★ Nappy bucket, or plastic bag to dispose of nappy.
★ Clean nappy and liner.

How to change a nappy

1. Nappies should be changed before or after feeds, and whenever the area is wet or dirty — unless the baby

is happily sleeping, in which case the job can wait.

2. If there is a liner, remove it. Now take off the dirty nappy, and wipe the worst of the mess off the baby with a tissue or cotton wool, perhaps also using baby lotion. Wipe towards the bottom, not away from it, to keep dirt away from the penis, vagina or bladder.

3. Now clean the baby well with cotton wool and warm water, drying the area carefully afterwards.

4. You may put on some protective cream like castor oil cream but if the baby is changed regularly and is comfortable, this is not necessary.

5. Put on the clean nappy. This is easy with a disposable nappy (make sure it is tight, though) and trickier with a terylene one. For these, fold the nappy into a triangle and bring one corner up between the baby's legs, the others either side of its hips, carefully securing the lot with a nappy pin. Keep the pin attached to your clothes and not lying around where it could hurt the baby.

6. Wash your hands with soap and water.

NAPPY RASH

You may notice a rash or a little redness on the skin in contact with the nappy. Make sure you are cleaning your baby thoroughly. Change nappies more frequently for a while to reduce the possibility of a wet or dirty nappy coming in contact with the sore skin. There are plenty of protective creams available to treat the soreness, and it is a good idea to let the baby lie on an untied nappy for a while to give the affected area some fresh air and sunlight. If the condition doesn't clear up, consult your doctor.

BATHING A BABY

Bathing a baby can be great fun, or awful, depending on whether or not your baby objects to getting wet. You may have purchased a baby bath (which bears a suspiciously close resemblance to a washing up bowl — so why not just that?), or you may choose to bathe your child in the sink for the few months before it can be put in a shallow bath. Watch out for the taps in the sink — you may bang yourself or the baby on them.

Make sure the water is not too warm for a baby's sensitive skin by testing it against your cheek or on your elbow. Use a sponge, no soap, and don't let go of the baby, and you can't go far wrong. Make sure the baby is quickly dried and put back into warm clothes. Don't forget that any amount of water can be dangerous to a baby. NEVER leave a baby unattended, even for a minute, while bathing him or her.

SLEEPING

For the first few months the child should sleep in its parents' room. That way its needs can be met quickly and the parents can rest assured that the baby is safe. Babies should sleep on their backs with head facing to one side. This way they can kick off bedclothes if they feel too hot. They should never be given pillows as they may suffocate on them.

If you find your work is beginning to suffer for lack of sleep you may decide to sleep in a separate room, or on the couch, for a couple of weeks. Many couples resort to different sleeping arrangements for a few weeks. Talk about it with your partner first though.

SLEEPING AND FEEDING TIMES

Every baby is different, and there is no 'normal' pattern for sleeping or feeding. Most babies start by wanting a feed every 2–3 hours (it can be less through the night), but a routine of less frequent feeds soon emerges and by two months most babies only need five feeds a day. Sleeping patterns are equally unpredictable. Some perfect babies sleep through the night from early on, others wake every two hours, non stop. Newborn babies sleep for up to half the hours in the day, in whatever pattern they find comfortable. Establish a routine, and *never* play lively games with a baby in the middle of the night — it will learn that 3 a.m. is playtime!

THE BABY'S HEALTH

Cot death is a danger that may be on your mind. It afflicts a tiny minority of families (two out of every 1,000 babies under the age of one). Some experts suggest these mysterious deaths are caused by the baby simply forgetting to breathe or overheating, others that the cause is suffocation by bedding, or toxic fumes from mattress stuffing. All you can do is check the baby regularly, and avoid putting anything that could choke or suffocate the baby in the cot.

Cot death is just one of a number of inevitable worries you and your partner will have in these early days. Some parents panic every time their child coughs, their natural concern amplified by the vulnerability of babies. Clearly if you are concerned about your child's health you must visit or call a doctor.

POST NATAL DEPRESSION

Early weeks with a baby can be a tiring and worrying time, and some women suffer badly from post natal depression, which is a sense of uselessness and fatigue. You may find your partner suffers this one day but not on others. Do your best to reassure her that she is coping well and that you are both going to enjoy parenthood. If your partner's depression continues, and particularly if she is not sleeping well, you may need to talk to her doctor.

SEX AFTER PREGNANCY

The time couples take to resume sexual relations after a birth varies enormously from weeks to many months. If your partner had a difficult birth, use of forceps or an episiotomy, intercourse may be painful. Once penetration has hurt, she will fear it the next time — and so an unhappy cycle of pain commences. She will be drier for a while so use a vaginal lubricant to make things easier. Fatigue may reduce both, or one of your, sex drives anyway, and you may feel inhibited if the baby is in the room. As has been stressed throughout this book, communication is the key to solving any problems, and some men seem to have great difficulty talking about sex with their partner. But silence leads to misunderstanding and that will worsen the problem.

One myth about breast feeding is that it prevents conception. This is not the case and when you resume intercourse you will need to commence contraception, which may be a shock after the past year of not having to bother. If your partner was on the Pill, she may choose to start taking it again. If she used a diaphragm, she will need to be fitted with a new one. Get advice from a doctor on this.

Chapter 8

LIFE GOES ON

Nine months is a long time. But it is only a few hours in a waiting room compared to the lifetime of caring that you are now beginning with your child. Everything that involves the baby has to be planned so that its demands for food, clean clothes and comfort can be met. That can be pretty draining. But you have to look after yourself and your partner too: it is easy to fall permanently into the role of father, and neglect your lover, your work, and your other interests. Your priorities will have changed, but your personality will not. So this final chapter looks at the development of your child and how you can help it, and at the task of ensuring the rest of your needs are fulfilled too.

THE DEVELOPMENT OF A BABY

AT BIRTH, a baby can only focus on objects around 8–10 inches (20–25 cm) away. Bright lights are painful, and the enthusiastic father grinning from the other end of the room is no more than a blur. Ability to focus longer and shorter distances comes over the next four months.

A young baby will be able to follow moving objects such as car keys being swayed in front of its face, but will lose sight of them occasionally. After a couple of weeks the baby is able to tell some colours apart, and is most attracted to bold colours like red and blue.

It takes a week for a baby to recognise the smell of its mother's milk, and it already has a taste for sweet breast milk. Its hearing is quite sensitive and it will be startled by loud noises and soothed by soft murmurings. Babies hear the higher frequency of women's voices better than the deeper male tones. Babies can clutch things, but only if the object is put within their grasp. They let go when they are distracted by wanting to do something else — not as a conscious 'release' action.

AT ONE MONTH, a baby lying on a rug can lift its chin from the floor, and within a few weeks will be able to take a swipe at objects within range. Babies will smile in response to sounds such as tinkling bells and squeaky toys.

AT TWO MONTHS a baby can lift its head when it is lying flat, and will study whole objects, not just part of them, as its curiosity grows.

AT THREE MONTHS the baby can lift its shoulders, and can place its hands around objects to hold them (left or right handedness does not show until around three years of age). It may start making cooing noises from this age, and will quieten at the sound of a parent's voice. From now on babies respond better to stimulus and they show affection by smiling at whoever is looking after them. You may find you are jealous of some friend or relation getting the same warm smile as you during play, but babies are not very discriminating at this age and believe that everyone is there to cater for them!

SIX MONTHS may see the start of crawling, but not every baby even bothers to crawl — some roll for a while, then walk! They may also use furniture to pull themselves up to a standing position. The baby starts to make repetitive sounds like 'gaga'. Babies usually start to teeth at around five to six months.

TEN MONTHS is about the earliest a baby will start to

walk (although it could take another six months) and it can now feed itself easy-to-hold food such as fruit. The beginnings of speech appear as it starts to associate making certain sounds with certain things. At this stage a baby can voluntarily let go of objects.

BABY DEVELOPMENT — FOOD

Switching from breast milk onto solid food is something every baby does at a different time. At three to four months you can start trying the baby with solids, and usually by six months a baby will be accepting soft, gooey food from a spoon. Initially this will be in combination with breast feeding, but once the baby is used to the new way of eating, they can be weaned off the breast altogether.

If the food has been stored in the fridge, take the chill off it first — but there is no need to heat up these early meals. Baby food has to be soft as they cannot chew, and must not contain salt, as this quickly dehydrates a baby. Make eating fun by talking your baby through the movements as you gently pop the spoon into your child's mouth and draw it out again. Be sensitive to when the child has had enough and is rejecting more spoonfuls — do not get tempted into forcing another mouthful in.

BABY DEVELOPMENT — PLAY

Babies love to play, and parents seem to instinctively talk as they play, producing a running commentary of 'where is the ball? Here it is!' etc. This helps in speech development — babies learn a lot by habit, and if they find everyone else talks all the time, they will want to learn to talk too. The following guidance on play patterns may help:

★ Don't expect too much. You may want your child to be an engineer, but a pile of building bricks is for knocking down with a swipe, not discussing construction techniques.

★ Vary play — from picking up and dancing to sitting and watching small movements in a toy.

★ Time play carefully. An exciting game just before bedtime wakes up the baby who then has to be calmed down again before it will sleep.

★ Make a time for you to play. Fathers often find they get home from work eager to play with their child, and find it has just been playing and is exhausted. Set aside a period, say 7–8 p.m., when you are relaxed and can spend time with your child. Scheduling like this helps you both.

★ React a lot. A bored expression with one eye on the TV will not stimulate the baby as much as genuine interaction. Keep talking, commentating on what is happening.

BABY DEVELOPMENT — SLEEPING

In due course (the timescale varies with every baby and every parent) you should be able to put your baby's cot in its own room at night. Babies feel secure in a known environment, so make sure your baby is already familiar with its nursery, and move any toys that were in or attached to the cot in with it. These tips on creating a nursery may help:

★ Do not go overboard on wallpapering in bright colours or with children's cartoon characters — your baby will hardly notice. A few splashes of colour such as from pictures will be just as effective.

★ Keep the room warm and at a fairly constant temperature. Babies are vulnerable to the cold.

★ Have a low level light source such as a table lamp at

the far end of the room from the cot. Use a low wattage light bulb. This allows a soft, reassuring light in the room without glare or getting in the baby's eyes.

★ Mobiles hanging from the ceiling, especially above the cot, are great favourites with babies as they are attractive to look at as they move and good to play with.

★ Soothing noise, whether it be music or whale sounds, can help a baby sleep.

★ Babies lose heat through their heads and need to be kept in a room at a constant temperature of 70°F (20°C). A combination of heaters, clothing and bedding will keep the baby warm.

YOUR OTHER LIFE

However content you are with your new family, both you and your partner need to maintain some interests outside the home. Yours may come through contact with people at work, although you may have other places to socialise too. Your partner has probably stopped work at least for a while: encourage her to visit friends, join mother/baby groups, and get out on her own or with your regularly. Young babies will be quite safe with a competent sitter who knows how to feed and change them. You may not have had the time or energy for romance over the last few months, so make an effort now in whatever way you wish — flowers, candlelit dinners, days out, presents — you will know what your partner will enjoy. She deserves a break and some time with you.

From now on, you are sharing the role of parent with your partner, and there are many books giving practical advice and guidance on the development of your baby into a toddler and small adult. By all means read them to gather information, but instinct, common sense, and imagination are the essential requirements for a good parent, and you can't get them out of books.

WHAT KIND OF FATHER DO YOU WANT TO BE?

Everybody wants the best for their baby. For men, that means they want to be the best father in the world. But what does that mean? How do you learn to be a father? How do you know if you are doing it well? There are no easy answers to these questions, and there is no 'right' way to be a father, but you can find out a lot about the kind of father you want to be by thinking the whole thing through.

We have a role model to work from: our own fathers. In fact it seems most men feel very strongly that they do *not* want to be like their own fathers. The most common complaint is that their fathers were never there — they were always out or doing things from which their son was excluded.

The whole idea of what a father is has changed dramatically over the years. The Victorians believed the father should be a figure of authority, a disciplinarian, a provider. Today, fathers are expected to play with their children as part of an active role within the family, to be a source of fun as well as (in many cases) supplying most of the money to run the household.

The longer a father and child are together, the closer their relationship is likely to be. However much you want this, it can be difficult. Your job may keep you from the home until your child is asleep for the night. There will be times when you have to choose between doing your job and seeing your child — and whichever you decide, you are bound to feel a little guilty about it. You may find that for every few minutes you have to play with your child there are many other tasks to be done. It may help if you consciously make a time when you see your child, perhaps for an hour in the evening and again the next morning. Maybe you always bath the baby, or you share the job equally with your partner. Try not to compete with your partner for your baby's love, by trying to do everything because you are jealous of their close relationship.

You may find that you are forced into an authoritarian role. Many exasperated mothers have warned a mis-behaving child to 'wait until your father gets home'. As he arrives home, with a sunny smile and a surprise present for his child, he is expected to transform himself into a stern, admonishing parent. It is worth agreeing a few ground rules with your partner on this early on: are you prepared to be used as a threat in this way? Are you prepared to smack your child or do you think physical violence solves nothing? Good communi-cation between parents brings harmony and stability which helps form a secure home and a happy environment for your child.

Some men find they become authoritarian, partly because they do not understand children. Identifying obedience with respect, they set demandingly high standards of behaviour with no licence for experimenta-tion. Do not allow yourself to be turned into an intimidating bully.

You will undoubtedly make a better father if you enjoy the role, and do not resent the time or the effort of parenthood. Look for benefits in all the experiences of fatherhood, share the joys and the worries with your partner, and you will help to build a happy family.

USEFUL ADDRESSES

The Family Planning Association
27–35 Mortimer Street
London W1N 7RJ

British Pregnancy Advisory Service
Guildhall Buildings
Navigation Street
Birmingham B2 4BT

National Childbirth Trust
Alexandra House
Oldham Terrace
London W3 6NH

Child Benefit Centre
DSS
Newcastle upon Tyne
NE88 1AA

Gingerbread
35 Wellington Street
London WC2E 7BN

National Childminding Association
8 Masons Hill
Bromley
Kent BR2 9EY

Family Credit Unit
DSS
FREEPOST
Government Buildings
Warbeck Hill
Blackpool
FY2 02F

GLOSSARY

Abortion Induced or spontaneous delivery of the foetus.

Afterbirth See placenta.

Amniocentesis Test in which a small amount of amniotic fluid is removed from around the baby while it is still in the womb and checked for the possibility of Downs Syndrome or other disorders, usually in babies of older women.

Amniotomy Artificial breaking of the amniotic sac.

Anaemia A blood disorder caused by lack of red blood cells to carry oxygen.

Anaesthetic A way of causing loss of sensation (to avoid pain) which can be applied locally or generally.

Ante natal The months of pregnancy.

Birth canal The vagina during birth.

Braxton-Hicks contractions Contractions which can occur during the pregnancy and which do not signal the start of birth.

Caesarian delivery Operation to remove baby from womb via a cut in the mother's abdomen.

Cervix The bottom, or neck, of the womb.

Chromosomes Minute structures which contain the genes carrying hereditary characteristics.

Colostrum The first milk produced by the breasts, which is particularly high in proteins and antibodies to protect the baby.

Contractions Tightening of muscles around the womb which open up the cervix and then deliver the baby.

Couvade (From the French couver, to brood) Physical symptoms in the male during pregnancy, caused by anxiety.

Crowning The appearance of the baby's head in the vagina.

Embryo The name for the baby up to its seventh week in the womb, after which it is known as the foetus.

Enema Emptying the bowels with warm soapy water.

Epidural Use of anaesthetic in the lower spine to cut off pain from the lower half of the body during birth.

Episiotomy Cut made between the vagina and anus to ease birth.

Fallopian tubes The two tubes which link the ovaries to the uterus.

Foetus (also spelt Fetus) The term for the baby from seven weeks to birth.

Fontanelles Soft parts between bits of the baby's skull before it completely joins together.

Guthrie Test A blood test carried out on babies after a few days to check for mental handicap.

Gynaecologist Doctor specialising in women's health.

Haemorrhage Bleeding.

Hormones Body chemicals.

Hypertension High blood pressure.

Hypotension Low blood pressure.

Intravenous drip Way of giving liquid food or other substances to the body via a tube inserted in a vein.

Jaundice Condition caused by a fault in the liver, making the skin look yellow.

Lactation Production of milk for breast feeding.

Lanugo Hair which grows on the foetus in the womb which mostly disappears before birth.

Linea nigra A dark line along the abdomen during

pregnancy which fades after the birth.

Meconium   First bowel excretion by the baby.

Midwife   Nurse who deals with pregnancy, labour and delivery.

Miscarriage   Spontaneous premature delivery of the foetus or embryo.

Nausea   Feeling of sickness.

Obstetrician   Doctor specialising in dealing with pregnancy.

Oestrogen   Female sex hormone.

Ovulation   Release of the female egg from an ovary.

Oxytoxin   Hormone used to stimulate contractions.

Paediatrician   Doctor specialising in care of babies and small children.

Placenta, or afterbirth. Lining of the womb which carries nourishment and oxygen to the baby and which is released after the birth.

Post natal   The time after the birth.

Pre-eclampsia or Toxaemia   Condition which can occur in pregnancy and is shown by high blood pressure.

Premature birth   Baby born before the 37th week of pregnancy, usually weighing less than 5½ lb (2.5 kg).

Primigravida   Medical term for first time mother prior to the birth.

Progesterone   A hormone produced by the ovaries.

Puerperium   The 4–6 weeks following the childbirth.

Rhesus factor   A factor found in red blood corpuscles. Blood is either Rhesus positive or Rhesus negative.

Sperm   Male seeds ejaculated at orgasm one of which may fertilise the female egg.

Ultrasound scan   Picture of the foetus made with high frequency sound waves.

Umbilical cord   The cord linking the baby to the placenta.

Uterus   The womb, a pear shaped organ which

enlarges during pregnancy as the baby grows.

Vagina Passage leading from the outside to the uterus.

Vasectomy Operation for male sterilisation.

Vernix Waxy white protective coating formed on the foetus and sometimes still apparent at birth.

Womb See uterus.

INDEX